in the gray

sia shete

AOS PUBLISHING, 2024

AOS POETRY, 2024

Copyright © 2024 Sia Shete

Sia Shete

ISBN: 978-1-990496-21-9

Cover Design: Jessica James

Visit AOS Publishing's website:
www.aospublishing.com

INTRODUCTION

For every person who grew up only knowing survival, every elder sister who became a guardian, every hopeless romantic who keeps believing and every woman who keeps being told she's not enough.

These broken pieces that you are made of, are beautiful. Just like a shard of broken glass.

I hope you embrace your flaws, for they make you beautiful.

with hope and love,
ss.

Foreword

A rainy afternoon. A warm cappuccino. A gushing stream of tears. And a broken heart. Not because of a love once found and lost like a little child's fading smile, but like the love that was snatched away, by those who raised you. That's how this book came into existence.

A never ending void is something a majority of us will always feel, never to be mended. All we can do is bring the sun to a rainy day by letting our emotions out. By feeling. By letting our guard down. But how do you let your guard down when your walls are so high? When he who broke your heart rests so peacefully in the graveyard of your mind? How do you delete from existence every single memory? Or, more importantly, how do you decide if you really want to?

You don't. You'll never want to, but sometime or other you're going to have to. Let go. For you. For the younger version of you who craved peace, love, happiness and pure joy. You owe it to yourself.

My dear readers. Or, rather. My dear travelers. That's what we all are aren't we? Travelers? Wandering everyday from one day to another, one thought to another and one emotion to another. So, my dear travelers:

Here is a message to you as you delve deeper into this ocean of endless emotions. It may not be okay for a really long time, it may get harder, it may tear you apart like the roaring thunder in the gray sky.

But I plead.

Stay.

Stay, for the suns yet to rise. They are expecting you. Stay, for the flowers yet to blossom. They crave your touch. Stay, for the saplings unborn. They wish to be nurtured by you. Stay, for the places unseen wish to be gazed at, by you. Stay, for the woman who stayed for you. Stay, for the wick of the candle that waits for you to blow the flame out. Stay, for the stars that wouldn't be as bright without you. Stay, for the lover you haven't come across yet, but who spends hours thinking about the ghost of you. Stay. Survive. Surrender, but only to the life, that came with you, that you came with.

Stay, for a million eyes that havent seen you yet, and would regret never having seen you. Stay and hold on, though it will hurt. Everything does. But it is only you, who can choose what kind of hurt you want to put yourself through. It is you, who will choose who lets you feel low.

It all comes down to you.

Fight.

Stay.

Hold on.

You are loved. By something in this universe, that does not care about your shape, size, gender, the color of your skin, your race, but sees the universe in your eyes.

You are loved.

Dedicated to my grandfather who looks at me wherever he is, happily and hopefully proud, whom I will be eternally grateful to for the rest of my life.

i. sire

even not being with you physically, makes me feel like home,
every inch of you, every part of you my arms and adoration
wants to roam.

you were the sunshine that was hiding behind the dark clouds,
you are the only one I'd want to dance with in the middle of
large crowds.

everyday you hold me from afar, you're the reason I stay sane,
without you this existence would be like a grassland without the
rain.

my time before you was liveable, my life before you was just
fine,
but when you appeared into my life you became my safe place
and my shrine.

every hour without you is getting tough and it will get tougher,
but for the future and beyond with you, this chest aching pain
I'm ready to suffer.

i used to close my eyes and all I could see was darkness,
I felt empty, I felt hollow,
but at this very moment, your hand in mine as we walk under
the streetlights with doughnuts, rushing home, is the thought I
want to follow.

life without you was going on

life without you was like a stroll through the woods,
but now that you're here, it's like the hidden lake in the middle
of the forest I knew existed,
oh how your face through digital mediums makes my heart go
haywire, it's twisted.

thank you for holding me and carrying me through the fire,
even though you are ten thousand miles away, this bond with
you is a sire.

hold on, don't let go, love me, heal me,
let's forget the world even exists and spend eternity together,
people will say there are better ones out there but for me you're
the heather.

this distance, bringing us closer, this love, everyday grows
fonder.
this love is new, but this feeling is foreign,
my heart never ached for someone like it does for you,
on a cloudy, misty morning, on a delicate blade of grass, you're
the drop of dew.

we have a long way to go, we have good times to look forward
to,
it's a long way down, but you are the only person to whom I
want to say "I do."

ii. myrtle and mirth

the waves swept the shore.
the rain poured and we smelled the petrichor.

you held my hand and lay a kiss.
my corset waiting to be put on, I took a risk.
a vision of small feet and us with the batter we're waiting to
whisk.

the waves are increasing, colliding with the rocks.
we're trapped in our bodies, but we can see the blood stained
frocks.
pin drop incessant cries. loud screams and tiny feet all around,
confusion and chaos.
τι χάσιμο δακρύων, δολοφονία πατού.

the waves were furious. Poseidon, waiting to punish the
uninvited guest.
i remember, once ripening, now weak hearts, giving us their
best.

what went wrong in what seems like a replica of the life we had?
everything was confusing, myrtle and mirth mixed like mad.
wishing compulsion would work, hoping I'd hit my head and
forget.
but all I would be left with, disconnect, cold and hatred.
deciding to hold your hand, I didn't.

Struggling to see the imperfections, you are full of stars,
A galaxy inside of you, the universe in your eyes,
Smooth skin, covered with an *ocean of scars.*
I held your hand for the final time and all I could feel were the
ghastly lies.

iii. decay and decompose

am I a doll broken beyond repair?

the glue isn't holding on anymore.
the polish is wearing out.

my porcelain skin is peeling off like weathered rocks.
a perfect hairdo, now looks like the leftover grass in the wildfire.

rosy red cheeks are still red but for *untethered reasons.*
the bow that perfectly sat on the lush redhead now rests with its
eyes shut on my lap.

delicate intricate shoes made with "everlasting" affection, well
what so damned came along the way, lying my way through
every sitting confession.

the others stared at me, like the upper class at the refugees.
their perfectly tied hair, lush eyes, and I remembered how mine
were pools of honey.
what I did to myself, the consequences to my actions, this little
creature lived her life being clumsy.

alas, as I decay and decompose into the earth, my eyes are
heavy not with tears but regret for here begins another ending.
for here begins another ending.

iv. tears and blood

safe haven. I resided. I believed.
mistaken or disappointed?

this is getting worse. I am unable to breathe.
a cold wave hits the shore but I want warmth.
lights fade, visions blurred, stars fall.
out for help, and in desperation, to you I call.

follow me into the cave. intrigued emotions, disappearing faces.
let me be a step ahead, but I am afraid when I look back you'll
be long gone,
the tide carries me to Atlantis, but I snap out and it's already
dawn.

weaklings suffer, die and disintegrate, strongest survive, adapt
and stay.
what hogwash had someone said.
if more, the weaklings survive and the strongest evaporate,
sluggish withdrawal occurs and life inside me hankering to
abate.

the moors call to me, the wolves howl in the wind.
everything seems different, the air is gray, in its voice, retaliating
to threats and screams,
of you, of me, of us, of our past,
a rumbling gamble in our fate shall never last.

lilies scathed, thunder rumbling, sky cries.
your own burnt epitaph scrapes out vulnerable lies.
forgive the sinned, forgive the unamused.

regardless of your existence, this world shall continue.

birds shall chirp, skies shall cry, thunder shall destroy any
evidence of you,
for today, tears and blood shall mix in the
most shrewd jew.

v. bonnie and clyde

a million days, a million nights,
a hundred thousand beautiful sights.

counting days, counting hours,
indulging in our dirtiest devours.

walking hand in hand, kissing like there's no tomorrow,
sadly we didn't know, here's where the world ends, drenched in
our own sorrow.

hands shake, acquaintances made, laughs shared and bodies
collide,
in a world of new lovers every night, we thought we were
Bonnie and Clyde.

unsolved mysteries, endless tears, affecting trauma and madness
hither,
sitting on the verge of our souls, in my hand a knife and yours, a
cither.

guess our intentions were divergent, only our bodies complied,
before the sun divorced the darkness, my dark side got you
crucified.

gently as I kissed you on the forehead one last time, to see if
you had left the realm or were still on the same as mine,
while you lived on and continued to take the spotlight, oh baby,
how could I shine?

that night broke me, murdering my own man,
weeping, drowning in your blood, engulfed in my demons,
suffocating on your incandescent smile playing in my mind,
my darling, you and I, every kiss, every intercourse, every lust,
every talk, was timed.

So here as I go, as I run away from the rancid smell, that leaves your body, as I run from the hate that grows within me, for myself,
oh my my, dear Lord, help me amend my impulsive decisions, make this wretched act of mine an elision.

as I leave this realm, eager to unite with my part time lover, to take him forever, to feel every inch of him, free from human cold, and guilt of what I did to him,
I know I will never be able to see him, for my flickering fate is so grim.

so here's to my man, here's to whom I betrayed,
as hell's wrath and the devil's fury does over me cascade.
does over me cascade...

vi. lies in me

i'm a wanderer. I'm a lost soul.
is it being human that makes me lost?
or is it being a wanderer that makes me lost?

i travel, i love but i am incapable of making one place my home.

my home lies in every shadow of the mountain,
my home lies in every breeze of the cold himalayan wind,
my home lies in every little sun's ray,
my home lies in every drop of ocean, in every drop of the sea
swaying silently,
my home lies in the little happiness and the grief of humanity,
my home lies in this concrete jungle,
my home lies in the blooming forests,
my home lies in morose poetry, the one that describes death
and afterlife,
my home lies in heaven, in hell, if that ceases to exist,
my home lies in this soil, in this very world,
my home lies in the little hands of the newborns and the
mothers cradling breasts,
my home lies in where i find nirvana, not where nirvana finds
me.

my home, lies in me.

vii. fire and ice

lights on, lights off,
stop, hold on, let me hear your breath.

let me see your curves, let me touch you like a dew on a leaf.
let me kiss your round, red lips, let me caress you.

let me hear you shudder and whisper in my ear, how much you
love me, and let me tell you how much I do, too.

let me put my hands where they're not supposed to be, let me
dance to your sound.
let me feel every inch of you, cause even then I won't get
enough of you.
let me take you to eternal elation and bring you to worldly
pleasure.

hold my hand, hold my head, hold this broken sapien and bring
her to life,
let this air between us fade and let there be nothing but your
body, infernally colliding with mine.

let me take you in completely, until I am full, until nothing but
short breaths escape me.
oh my darling, we are unearthly souls, journeying together to
find divinity.

all that grace, all that body, all that face,
makes me realize how this world's a race, and how you and I
are just two young cherubim trying to make it, wrapped in our
own cloaks.

you're the devil, I'm the angel, you're the angel, I'm the devil,
the surrounding, our hell, but do we fit in? maybe we don't, as
long as you're around I don't care.

I whisper your name we reach our peak,
the amalgamation of our bodies,
 the sweat of our lust,
the way your hands wrap in mine,
the way we stabilize our breath,
the way you look into my eyes and the way I look into yours,
a tear escapes me and a tear escapes you, as I remember the
times I wanted to talk
and you wouldn't,
for now I realize the conversations between your fingers and my
skin,
are the most important discussions we could have.

you and I are fire and ice,
up in flames when touched, numbing to bear.

viii. you

Stop chasing love, the right one won't run.
Stop expecting love, the correct ones will happen.

Last night, I heard a song that made me think of you, but when
the song ended, it made me think of you too.

I told you about my past, I expected you to exist in my future,
turns out the light can be turned off but it can't ever be
dimmed.

I guess I was too busy planning the ending, before analyzing the
journey.

 i was too caught up in planning the holidays, before making
sure we were really there.

i thought i was your vacation and your home, i thought i was
your medicine.
i thought.

but now, i've learned.
i've learned to forget the person, not the lessons.
they asked me how I knew it was over.

i said, "sometimes you miss the memories
more than the person."
that's when I knew this road ended. All roads do.

i pretended to be okay.

honestly, i hoped that you'd do more than just occupy the space
in my camera roll.

i hoped that you'd do more than just being a "him I loved" in my
diary.

 i hoped.

how can you call it love, when you're crying more than you're smiling?
how can you call it love when you're debating more than you're deciding?
how can you?

there is a difference between giving up and knowing that you've had enough.
clearly, the former worked better for you.

goodbyes hurt, but it's the unexpected ones that kill.
.
because you know what?
you were a whole different kind of poison.

the one covered with chocolate.
the one with a smooth surface.
the one that looks appealing.

you melt, and then the sweetness fades...
that's when your taste turns sickly sour.

you consumed me.
you.

ix. imprinted scar

here's to you.
the pillows were my safe place,
the bed was my warmth.
until I found you.

your arms became my safe place and your love my warmth.
but just like a linen bedding loses its glamor, so did you.

I regret not checking up on you, not making sure that you were
that same plain vanilla, an elegant linen.

I think somehow, your journey towards turning into a dusty old
cloth, never to be touched, was partly my fault.

I didn't take hints, nor did I pick up the clues.
a mortal combat, is what took place.

you and me, straight to the conclusions.
no discussions, no solutions, no questions, no anger, just a cold
war.

when I thought 'who could ever let me go' I was wrong.
I should have thought 'who could ever stay'.

you were that one person who did, and I let you go too, into the
thin, crisp, haunting, cold, cruel night air.

the universe told me to chase you, just like now, I chase my
scattered past.
 I chase it to once and for all get hold of you and never let you
go.

we were weird, we were dumb, we were inconstant, we were
atrocious, we were kids, still are, but that's human, right?

oh lover, wherever you are,
here I come to you, in my imagination, my car,
I am looking at the sun and you're looking at the moon, so far,
just to find you, stroking her hair at the bar.

I looked at myself, clothes tattered and dusty, just like the linen
I thought you were..
dancing with the ghost of your past, as you left me,
 with your long imprinted scar.
your long imprinted scar.

x. wake up

meet me tonight...

meet me tonight at the forest,
right near the glittering pond.
meet me tonight, put your best tux on.
meet me tonight, take me in your arms.
meet me tonight, where it's dry but on us it'll rain.

meet me tonight, where our hearts are fragile,
not the glass.
meet me tonight, between the dense pine trees, just to hear
nature's song.
meet me tonight, when I hold your hand, kiss it and in your
skin I'll drown.
meet me tonight, and all borders will come dwindling down.

meet me tonight, where love hurts, where love aches, but love
heals.
meet me tonight, where we know this relationship will break us,
but we're thankful for the endless lessons we needed.
meet me tonight, where our hearts are broken, where when we
hold hands we don't feel the spark anymore.

meet me tonight, where into the forest we vanish, to lose our
minds and find our souls.
meet me tonight, where we jump off the cliff and build our
wings on the way down.
meet me tonight, where kisses, hugs, and making love, are
nothing more than words.
meet me tonight, when they'll tell us to follow our hearts.
but if it's in a million pieces, which one do we follow?

meet me tonight, where I'm not afraid of love, but afraid of
being the only one who falls.
meet me tonight, where I breathe my last breath, yet it feels like
it's just the beginning.
meet me tonight, or watch me as I go.

because I was never there.
wake up, it's dawn.
the ghost of me fading at a distance, unable to let you go.

xi. myriad hues

mountain wind, mountains mist,
hoping nights would last longer, rooting the circumstance with a
closed fist.

gale gushing through my hair,
magic of the mountains calling my name,
people say this infatuation won't last,
in my heart I know I don't care,
the world will these menial things forget, but I will dust them as
they bloom in their frame.

myriad hues of the skies anigh, martyrs' tears trickling down as
rain guarding the nation from above,
battling the worst of enemies even beyond life, driven by love
and respect for the nation over a commanded behoove.

stranded lands, piercing cold winds, mild dew,
two tapestries to save but only one permitted to sew.

staring into the moon's gaze,
belittled by the stars' luster,
on ground and above, we'll toast to freedom, as we roar the war
cry in a cluster.

snowy peaks with avalanches strong, undisturbed birds flying
high,
fear not, for I will return and fight one more time if on the
battlefield I die.

we've been told the water is sweet, blood is thicker,
yet why does it feel that the water's heavier than the red liquid?

why are brothers and sisters made and not born?
why is the last breath not so important anymore and all that
matters is freedom?
why does love feel like a luxury?

where can I sit and cry for hours undisturbed?
    I remember it being a stable tempo, yet all I hear now
are cries, reverbed.

lying in the cold, the ice makes it's way to my mind, pinning
down my last expression,
with a heavy heart the ice wins this battle, while I lay helpless, in
its discretion.

xii. a concept

it's cold. the snow, the rain, the hail.
where do we go?

run into the woods? run to the small shelter?
a bleak fire lit inside the cabin.

we ran hand in hand, I shivered but it wasn't the cold.
drenched in rain, clouds scattered across the sky, pouring
heavily.

nothing for the next hundred miles just you and I.
the faded scent of your perfume, mixed with the petrichor.
my small uke in one hand and your hand in the other, fingertips
lighting my
skin with bumps.

hungry souls, intertwined in a knot,
the cold weather was long forgotten and suddenly everything
turned hot.
100 words. 20 sentences. 2 hearts beating.

so much to say, but your gaze did the work.

with the rain, was another salty substance mixed, as the candle
lit, and the fire went out, it escaped your hazel eyes.
you held me, closer than ever. I could hear your breath.
everything was lost in that moment, just you and I.

i drowned in the ocean inside your eyes. devoured every bit of
you and kept that little strand of hair away from your temple.

i felt like a helpless little child,
your skin was whiskey, definitely not mild.
the sun rose, the rain stopped, and you faded away,

i couldn't speak, everything froze,
and from my unfortunate bed, I rose.

xiii. sprinkle of imprecision

this seems like a meaningless affair, the kind you regret,
was it worth it? the will to live fades like the smoke out of a
cigarette.

thoughts intertwined like the roots of a banyan tree,
at least they have one another – I'm stranded, no one around to
set me free.

a slip case of mistaken identity, doesn't seem like a slip
anymore,
I'm the fish that kept swimming yet somehow was thrown
ashore.

a sixth sense and a hazy vision,
good enough to deceive them but all it needs is a sprinkle of
imprecision.

currents of the river stronger than ever, but the sediments
seemed to have vanished,
an attempt at redemption seems worthless, my image seems
tarnished.

xiv. sunshine and storms

feeling blue was supposed to be just an emotion,
from laughter to fading smiles, in a reverse gear goes the
promotion.

working one moment, losing hope in the next,
they ask me to talk to them but I can ever explain it on call, in
person or on text.

in a recurring cycle, the weather has plummeted from sunshine
to storms,
I stand alone naked, facing the faceless, while they wear the
same uniforms.

eyes filled with blood and veins filled with tears,
the pace is decreasing, from six to one, shifting gears.

my battery is running out, and so does my time,
every second alive makes me the criminal and living, the crime.

xv. new year's day

nightfall sets in and the darkness is where it's not supposed to
be.
a cacophony of owls and the night sounds haunt me.

the sun set a few hours ago when it wasn't
supposed to.
as I stroll through the dimly lit park, I see a
flickering light.

what would have made me write, now makes me cry.
the light flickers, just like the thread my existence hangs on.
soon, it goes off. a sign? an understanding? a dawning? I
wonder in utter confusion.

deciding against continuing to sit, I get up and keep pacing
through the now dark park.
an uncontrollable urge to call her ignites my body, but today, I
don't give in.

the surroundings smell like her. the surroundings seem like her.
a smell of nature sprinkled with a tinge of darkness. just right.
I keep walking. until I can see the streets. the dark and empty
streets of Louisiana at 3am.

it's a wonder really, how I craved the noise. the silence was too
loud for me.

ironically, as we fought for the last time, that's what she said and
set me free.
but was I free? or did I feel like I didn't want the freedom cause
I'd had too much of it?

new year's. I watched you enter the party, our friends didn't
change. you wore your usual sweatshirt. my usual sweatshirt.
confused. exhilarated. awkward. I grabbed a drink. sat by the
window and stared into the long night ahead.
I didn't see you until later, when everyone passed out, late at
night, only us, the yellow lights, the cold air, the pitch dark night
and the first of january.

cleaning up bottles and cups. together yet not together. how'd it
come to this, you became the stranger whose laugh I'd
recognise as you passed me on the wide Louisiana streets...
holding hands with that girl, the one I was worried about a few
months ago, when you were mine.

xvi. white lilies

"why didn't you say h-how bad it was?"
I did. every single day. every single second.

metaphors, cries and whatnot, he'd understand is what I'd
reckoned.

the look on his face was ghastly, tears escaped his eyes,
I lay there, blood flowing like a river out my body, it all came
back to me, hurt, heartbreaks and lies.

exhausted in this world, I am me in someone else's body,
breathing the air everyone else did, existing like a mere piece of
wood, seemed gaudy.

suffocating, and almost couldn't speak, "911, what's your
emergency?"
"my-m-my girlfriend is losing a lot of blood,"
his voice whispered shakily.

"please calm down. we are sending units, please tell me where
you are and stay calm,"
roared the personnel.
"147 and 36th, please, I beg you, hurry!"

he gazed at me, the same way he did on our first night.
when I saw the sparkle in his eyes and knew, one day I'd love
him with all my heart.

I shakily held his hand. "this is what's best for me. I couldn't
take it anymore. I have been choking for years, I thought it
would get better but it didn't. you, my love, are the reason I
lived. you are the reason I fought a bit more. but my time came
closer each day, there was nothing you could have done that
would have reversed that."

gasping for air, I tried to reach for his arm. he stroked my hair,
tears had now won the war.
he held me from underneath, trying to keep me awake.

police sirens sounded from the outside,
"just a few more minutes please,
pull through, you can do this,"
I was too tired to move.

I looked into his eyes, the glittering eyes had lost their sparkle,
dominated with worry and fear.

our eyes locked one last time.
"don't forget to send me white lilies,"
and that's when I felt numb.

xvii. pirouetted glass

"forget what I said."
my mind went numb.

the wine glasses in my hand, collided beautifully with the
marble and pirouetted to every inch of the room.

"forget what I said,"
his hoarse voice repeated.
"forget what?" my voice trying not to
break, squeakily replied.

he placed our bowls on the graphite counter, as he locked eyes
with me, it was as if he was mocking my act of the shattered
wine glasses.

"we never happened."

a chill went all through my body. my thoughts dating to the time
when I never understood why he loved me, came rushing back.
me, scared of almost every person, scared of the dark, scared of
opening up, scared that I'd be put down every time I confided
in someone, scared that I'd be left to rot like the dying flower in
the temple.

why did he love me?
was all of this just as minuscule as the flick of a switch for him?

"I need to go." he hurriedly placed the two bowls, packed his
stuff and rushed towards the door.

I ran as fast as I could, the transparent broken pieces of glass
made my feet their home. yet, I continued running. a red river
flowed through my living room.

I fell down to my knees, and held his thighs with my arms. but
he resisted. he insisted on going away. he couldn't stand the
sight of me.

"LET ME GO," he howled.

"you are my best friend. please don't leave I beg you."

"take care, I'm sorry." the words left his lips like they had no weight. they were just those. words.

my trembling voice squeaked.
he left and slammed the door in my face.

I sat there.

 right next to my allies.
the red river, the pirouetted glass pieces and coming back to square one, my darkest thoughts.

I was in pain. I was immune to the glass. but, the emotional one. I wanted answers. I didn't get them.

we needed one another. the chapter somehow closed way before it was supposed to begin.

I heard footsteps. it was him. I had them memorized.

he opened the door, looked at me, a tiny sparkle in his eye, lifted me up, tucked the one strand of hair just like he did on our first date, and kissed me.

and that's when I knew it was over.

xviii. bus ride

another long bus ride,
this journey lasts far too long,
in a black cardigan with the backpack by my side,
I close my eyes and it passes as though a two minute song.

passing streets, children munching on treats,
passing streets, children starving to death,
dancing on the endless, barren heaths,
only to collapse and draw one last breath.

buses pass by, seasons change,
thunder contaminates the clear skies,
your company left me weirdly deranged,
my lips sealed, for the world ignores my cries.

surrendering to an alternate reality,
envisioning the ride back home,
what hath caused such a wrecking calamity,
wandering every inch of soil,
before I mix with silt and loam.

xix. crimes in a foreign land

i sit on the veranda waiting for you to come,
i hopelessly wait, in regret I pour myself a rum.

i'm frightened of what you might do, I'm devastated for what
you might utter,
i try, yet you never allow my ears to slam their shutter.

i hopelessly wait, as you make your way from the land,
the land where you commit crimes, where all men do is stare,
they stand.

i'm unaware of this place, this foreign land where I can't go,
where I'm smacked when I step foot,
just like a tree isn't allowed to stay,
without you, the root.

i've been stripped. stripped off my rights.
i've been banned from experiencing those million, pleasing
sights.

my body craves touch, my skin craves fingertips,
sadly, all I get is my skin stuck in these little clips.

you leave before you arrive, my eyes water to convince you to
stay,
i'll never know if i'll be allowed to see the open skies beyond my
boundaries, what seems like a dreamy day.

xx. a door

a door.

 you and I walk in, suddenly everything seems familiar.
the feeling of a thousand suns flashing into our eyes, you and I
gaze at one another, like we did in a museum of art.
the sparkle seemed to grow deeper day in and day out. you held
me from behind. my heart raced. my heart ached.
tears rolled down my eyes and turned to pearls. they continued
to wet your sleeve.

I could feel you from behind, but I couldn't anymore. you were
right here. I turned around. you weren't anymore.
where did you disappear? were you just a figment of my
imagination?

I ran frantically around the house, my heart ran with me. my
mind seemed to stand still. I couldn't help but scream. scream
your name into the endless night.
my eyes bled. bled tears. I was all alone. you were there. right in
front of me. right behind me. I turned around once again. there
you were. trying to catch hold of me, trying to hold me close,
trying to brush your veiny hands through my hair.

but you couldn't.
you didn't try harder.
but you did.

I convinced myself all too well, that you didn't. for if I hadn't, I
would lay there, in the cold streets calling your name. waiting
for you to return, when I knew you wouldn't.

you constantly tried to collide your vanilla fingertips to my
harsh, dry face. the wind cutting my countenance. but the wind
eloped with you.

a goodbye.

a red car.

my body.

breathing.

yours beside me.

hand in hand.

cold.

xxi. north and south

there are days I feel as close to you as
the sky to the grass,
it thunders, it gets cold and in the end it gets
scorching hot,
midas said touch and be gold but I touch and
you turn to brass,
a desiccated body does slower than you rot.

plants sway to the wind blowing outside this storm,
we look at one another knife in hand,
your crimson blood, somewhat seems to form,
a shape, disfigured by poseidon, and you turn to timeless
granules of sand.

the sun sets in the east and rise in the west,
the ocean tides retrieve the dead fish thrown to the shore,
take cover, don't let them see you, a caged bird set free yet
under arrest,
stranded on an island, a single piece of wood and you grabbed
the oar.

undermining your ability to snatch my own life away,
clothes all tattered and torn, all you had to work was your
mouth,
the moon and stars gazed at us in hiding that day,
one last time, one last struggle, you'll go north and I'll disappear
into the south.